Our Sunday Visitor's
Christmas Memories

Our Sunday Visitor Publishing Division
Our Sunday Visitor, Inc.
Huntington, Indiana 46750

ISBN: 0-87973-919-3
LCCCN: 97-67611

Cover design by Monica Watts

Printed in the United States of America

919

Preface:
Memories of Christmas

Each year, when the nights are cold and the days are short, Christians gather together to remember and relive the Christmas story. The Gospels of Luke and Matthew tell a tale full of mystery and surprise. A child is born in an obscure corner of a poor land. He is a child like other children; his parents are people like us; his times are troubled as ours are; the circumstances of his birth — humble, inconvenient, secluded — familiar. Yet the Child was God Himself. His coming divided human history into two parts — that which came before His birth and that which comes after it. He is the center of our faith. And the annual feast of Christmas has become both a spiritual and a social focal point. It's an occasion to gather as families and communities to remember the coming of Jesus.

Each fall since 1984, the editors of *Our Sunday Visitor*, a weekly national Catholic newspaper, have asked readers to send in their most vivid and meaningful Christmas memories. The editors have published as many of these as they can in a special section of the newspaper each December. This book is a selection of these memories.

They are as rich and diverse as the story of Christmas itself. We read of acts of kindness and generosity, of gift-giving and sharing, of thankfulness and healing. Some memories are poignant; some are funny. Christmas is a time for families to gather — in joy but also in sorrow. Some of the stories collected here remind us of the pain of the first Christmas: poor travelers without shelter; an untimely birth in a place where

animals lived; a man, woman, and child who became refugees to flee a murderous tyrant; a child destined for execution.

The darkness of our world is part of the Christmas story, just as our celebration of Christmas occurs in the dark of winter. Yet at Mass we mark Christ's birth with words: "The light shines in the darkness, and the darkness has not overcome it." These memories testify to the eternal truth of that ringing affirmation. The light of Christ shines in His people, and it is reflected in their memories of Christmas.

The Editors of Our Sunday Visitor

A forever memory

May I always remember it:

Our front parlor is curtained off from floor to ceiling. We children are lined up for the grand Christmas-morning entry. I'm seven years old, sixth one from the top, sensing for the first time how in tune with one another we are. Theodore has just raced back downstairs with his necktie. Margery keeps humming the carol we've chosen for the procession. James and John, in Charlie Chaplin style, step in and out of place, tipping their imaginary derbies. David is smiling; this afternoon he'll be wearing his first pair of long pants. Eleanor and I are smoothing down our look-alike dresses. And now Robert is ready, his little hands receiving the infant figure, his golden curls vibrating with responsibility. As our song gains a bit of volume, Mama opens the curtain.

Oh, let it all remain forever as we saw it then — the very air alive with color, the dazzling tree, the manger scene completed, and, among the gifts, eight pairs of shiny new shoes.

Catherine Morissey
Dunkirk, New York

"Don't jump"

My first Christmas as a priest was not at all what I had expected. The altar-boy rehearsal for Midnight Mass conflicted with the work of the Altar Guild. Confessions, both afternoon and evening, were long and tiring, leaving little time to prepare the Christmas homily. There was standingroom only at the Midnight Mass, but the participation was minimal for the many young couples in attendance, who were on their way to other celebrations. On Christmas morning it seemed that every baby in the parish was at every Mass.

Following the last Mass, the pastor suggested that I make a hurried-up visit to my family home and be back so that he would be free for his family obligations to brothers and sisters. This led to my mother having to change the dinner hour in order to accommodate me in the family plans. So, tired and weary, I began my return journey to the parish. As I approached the top of a steep bridge, stretching four hundred feet above the harbor waters, a guard stepped out in front of my car and singled me to get out of the car. A man was poised to jump. He had climbed over the rail and stood on the narrow ledge.

I prayed! I called out, "Stop! God loves you very much! I am a priest. I can help you — please don't jump!"

His eyes cleared and he took my hand! Thank God!

The morning paper on December 26, 1962, featured two photographs on the front page: Pope John XXIII visiting a child in an orphanage in Rome, and a young priest joining hands with a troubled person on a bridge. The headline read: "How Some People Spent Christmas." What a great Christmas for me — I have never forgotten it.

Father John J. Geoghan
Weston, Massachusetts

The final shut-off

My boyfriend and I both had jobs, and I was living with my parents, so we were better off than most people in town during the Depression year of 1931. We decided to do something for a poor family at Christmas. I was a cashier at the gas company. I knew who the poor families were because they would come in regularly to beg that their gas be left on, even though they could not pay fifty cents on their overdue bill. I picked out a family that was more than five months overdue on its bill and whose gas was going to be shut off the day after Christmas.

We bought a Christmas tree, decorations, and lights. We bought presents for each member of the family, wrapped the gifts attractively, and then bought food — a turkey and a ham, vegetables, Christmas candy, bread, and a box of my mother's beautiful, cut-out, frosted, Christmas cookies.

When we arrived at the family's house on Christmas Eve, my boyfriend and I noticed that the blinds were all pulled to the bottom. We rang and rang the bell; after a long time, one of the children peaked out from behind a window shade. When they saw our arms filled with Christmas gifts and a Christmas tree, they opened the door. We walked into a living room completely devoid of furniture or rugs. In the kitchen was a stove and an empty icebox with the doors open. The kitchen table had orange crates around it. In the bedroom, there were mattresses on the floor, but no furniture. Everything had been sold off, piece by piece, to buy food.

They were overjoyed to see us, and the children started decorating the Christmas tree. The mother carried the groceries to the kitchen with tears in her eyes. We chatted awhile and then got up to leave.

The father of the family walked out to the car with us. Weeping, he told us that he had sealed all the windows and doors in the house. That night, when everyone was asleep, he had planned to turn the gas on so that he and his family would die peacefully.

We were stunned. We emptied our pockets of all the money we had — seven and a half dollars. We promised more help, and got it. Through our efforts, my parents and their friends hired the poor man for yard work and odd jobs. He eventually had a successful gardening business. We collected furniture for their home. What could bring more Christmas joy than saving the lives of five fine people?

Mildred H. Rudaick
Marysville, California

Beloved one of Mary

My husband and I have always wanted to have children but we had had great difficulty doing so. After eight years of treatment by fertility specialists, I finally conceived. But it was a difficult, high-risk pregnancy. After four months, we had one of the greatest disappointments of our married lives — we lost our baby. We had become discouraged and disillusioned with the treatments and tests for infertility — and with our faith somewhat.

A year after our loss, we decided to apply for adoption through a local Catholic agency. We began three-and-a-half years of counseling, parenting classes, and seminars to prepare us.

On the Wednesday before Mother's Day in 1988, we received our child, a daughter. But before we did, we had agreed to risk placement, which means that a child is placed in your home until the birth parents decide to place their child for adoption.

After six long weeks, our daughter's birth parents terminated their rights. But our daughter was still not legally ours. We had to wait another six months before her adoption was scheduled.

Our daughter, Carissa Marie, which means "Beloved one of Mary," was legally adopted on December 21. She was the greatest Christmas gift we could have ever received. Our love for our daughter is the kind of love we perceive the Lord's love is for us all: consuming and unconditional.

Jeannie Vig
Huntington, West Virginia

Hot line

For many years, I had taken calls on a crisis-pregnancy hot line from women looking for alternatives to abortion. One evening near Christmas, I was asked to return a call to someone who wanted to talk to no one except "Pat" — me. I reached a lady in the maternity ward of a local hospital. She identified herself as a caller I had spoken to approximately seven months earlier.

She had called our hot line by mistake, thinking that she could schedule an abortion. I had talked to her at great length. She had been worried about her age; I told her that I had my first child at the same age. She already had two boys; I had asked her how she would feel if this was the little girl she had always wanted.

She was calling to thank me. She had just given birth to a beautiful baby girl. This was the only girl on both sides of the family, and both she and her husband were ecstatic!

After I hung up the phone, with tears of joy in my eyes, I told my husband that I didn't need another thing for Christmas. These were the special moments that made it all worth while.

Pat Grimes
Pittsburgh, Pennsylvania

The great escape

I was but a little girl when my parents made their great escape from Communist Hungary through the heavily forested Vienna Woods, towing behind eight hungry little children.

It was dark in the woods; we had been walking all night. God must have been watching us very closely, for as daybreak approached and our tired little bodies were swaying with exhaustion, there appeared through the thickets two Austrian farmers behind a horse-drawn wagon. Our joy at this sight was indescribable. We hugged one another and danced and cried, and the little ones just stood there, shivering in awe. Wearily we piled into the creaky wagon and drifted off to a deep sleep to the soothing lullaby of Christmas songs bellowed out happily by our drivers. Our journey to freedom had blossomed into reality amidst that cold, gray dawn of Christmas morning.

As we approached the village nestled below the snowcapped mountains, we awoke to the sound of church bells ringing out "Silent Night." It echoed over hundreds of makeshift tents in a refugee camp scattered below us. I saw throngs of people and children laboring their way through the drifts of snow, and I heard laughter and songs fill the air. Eagerly we joined them, embracing and exchanging the news of our escape, united in spirit and ever so thankful.

The many years of oppression had been suddenly lifted from our lives and we were blessed with the most wonderful Christmas gift of all, freedom to yearn and fulfill the heart, mind, and soul in beautiful America, where we were received with open arms, provided a home, and given opportunities beyond our dreams.

Marianna Doan
Arlington, Texas

Make mine coffee

On Christmas Day 1936, my life was changed forever.

I was ten years old. We went to Midnight Mass. After Mass, we hurried home under the cold and starry night to a warm but meager "Depression Christmas" celebration. My aunts and uncles gathered at our house that year because my father was the only one of them gainfully employed in those hard times.

Along about 2:30 or so in the wee hours of Christmas morning, my father plucked a brown paper bag from the top shelf of the kitchen cupboard, pouring little dollops of reddish-purple liquid into glasses for the Big People. I didn't know it then, but it was port wine.

Almost as an afterthought, he offered me a mouthful or so in a little glass. "Merry Christmas," Poppa intoned solemnly, and they all responded in kind, with a Gaelic phrase or two sprinkled in. Then they quickly downed the contents of their glasses. So I did likewise.

And my life was changed forever. I sensed a euphoria that defied description, and I trembled, faint with awe for the strange sensation that I knew must be sinful because it felt too good not to be. I remember thinking that though I was ten years old, I was ten feet tall, able to leap tall buildings with a single drink. I giggled. I didn't know it, but I was drunk. Almost instantly. I vaguely remember floating into the living room and interrupting the Big People with some ridiculous remark while staggering visibly.

My parents, shocked, sent me quickly to bed, but all I remember was lying on a downy soft cottony cloud, all my cares and woes gone forever. I was happy and comfortable at last.

I thought I had finally discovered peace. But there was no peace. What I had really discovered was the cunning, baffling,

powerful world of the alcoholic. I had had my first drink, my first drunk, my first blackout, my first anti-social behavior; a pattern to be repeated for the next thirty-six years of my alcoholic nightmare.

In 1972 came sobriety and its true inner peace and joy.

A glass of wine? No thank you. Make mine coffee.

And Merry Christmas! Peace at last!

Jack O'Neil
Sewickley, Pennsylvania

The Jewish Christmas tree

I was thirteen years old at Christmas 1967. My father and I were struggling over religion. My father was Jewish and he had raised me to be a devout Jew, believing in the Old Testament as the Word of God. But during my religious instruction I had discovered the new way of life through Jesus Christ, the Son of God. My father was worried sick over me leaving his religion. I was pulling away from the "old" way in which he thought I should conduct my religious affairs. That year we spent many evenings debating my new-found faith.

As the end of the year approached and Christmas drew near, we still had not agreed about which religion I should practice. The turning point came shortly before Christmas. I asked my father if I could have a small Christmas tree. He looked at me with love, and I suppose at that moment he knew that I was committed to my new religion.

He agreed to a tree, but with conditions. The tree had to be small, white, and decorated with only blue bulbs. White and blue — the Jewish colors for royalty.

So as that royal Christmas tree stood on a tiny table in my father's house, we were at peace. The debate had ended.

Standing side by side, Jew and soon-to-be Catholic, we looked upon that little tree, and it became a symbol of hope and thanksgiving: my father's hope in the Messianic King, and my thanks to God for giving me a father who loved his daughter enough to allow her little Christmas tree to stand under a Jewish roof.

Pamela Sara Adreme
Hobbs, New Mexico

A screaming eagle

At Christmas 1985 we were looking forward to the return of our twenty-two-year-old son, Mark, who would be home on Christmas leave after six months of duty overseas. We were planning Christmas at Mark's favorite place, our lake home in Santee-Cooper County, South Carolina. He kept reminding us to bring his rifle, as he was looking forward to going hunting with his cousin Allen. He wanted to be with all the people he loved the most: his parents, sister, and grandparents.

Mark was scheduled to land in the United States in the early hours of December 12. As I was leaving the house for work that morning, my husband, LeRoy, said that the TV news was reporting that a plane from Germany had crashed in Canada. Military personnel and dependents were said to be on board. More details came. They said the plane was from the Sinai, and our Mark was coming home from six months peace-keeping duty in the Sinai. I went to work and called our prayer line and the churches and asked them to pray that Mark was not on that plane.

But he had been on it. Sergeant Mark Edward Carter and two hundred forty seven other soldiers of the 101st Airborne Division, "The Screaming Eagles," had died that morning in a plane crash at Gander, Newfoundland.

For me, Christmas is no longer that once-a-year time with decorated trees, carols, shopping, gifts, parties, and, oh yes, when Jesus comes for an hour at Christmas Mass. Christmas now is a time to work at seeing Christ in others; to share the joys and especially the sorrows of others; and to wish for all people, brothers and sisters in Christ, His peace and love, the greatest of gifts, for every single day.

Mary Lou Carter
Fayetteville, North Carolina

A good hair day

During the Korean War, I was living on a farm in Missouri with my husband, son, and daughter. Money was very scarce and Christmas was upon us. The livestock were out of feed, but our pantry was full of canned homegrown vegetables, fruits, pickles, jams, and jellies. I felt the Lord had provided our needs, as He promised. But my children's "wants" and the livestock's feed were foremost in my prayers.

Then an unusual ad came in the mail; a manufacturer wanted hair for the making of the Norden bombsight. I thought my hair looked good. I had a lot of it. I wore it in a double coronet braid on top of my head, but it was three inches above my ankles when I let it down. I went to the address in the ad, gave a sample of my hair, and waited. A lady came out and said, "Your hair is of the perfect tensile strength we need. Will you sell it?" I didn't hesitate. They cut it off, leaving three inches, and paid me thirty dollars.

I bought livestock feed, gifts for my children, and sugar and flour so I could make Christmas cookies and candies for my little ones. When I got home, the children didn't recognize me because I wasn't wearing my "crown." I explained the best I could what had happened.

To this day, my children remember, and remind me, of that Christmas when I let my hair down.

Doris F. Baker
Wichita, Kansas

The simplest things

I hadn't been able to go to Midnight Mass for years because I had to care for young children. When I finally decided I could manage it, the bishop had divided our parish to form a new one, and all we had for a church was a Quonset hut. I will never forget walking through the falling light snow and walking into that hut.

Walking into one of the beautiful cathedrals of the world could not compare with it. I felt as if I were truly kneeling in the stable, which only goes to show that the simplest things sometimes are the best. The infant Jesus was truly present that night.

Monica Daloia
Bay Shore, New York

Fröhliche Weihnachten!

I stood in the prison chapel watching visitors admire the Nativity scene. It was Christmas 1944. I was one of a group of German prisoners of war who had created the Nativity scene in Camp White, Oregon, and I was proud of my work and thankful to be where I was.

As a young draftee into the German army during World War II, I saw battle in Le Havre, Cherbourg, and Normandy. I was captured by Canadians on August 8, 1944, near Caen, sent to England, then to America. We were loaded onto transport ships, crossed the Atlantic in ten days and were brought ashore in New York, from where we were transported under heavy guard by train to Oregon. We were housed in two-story barracks, fenced in on all sides, with manned watchtowers in all four corners. The interior of one of the buildings had been converted into a chapel, with upstairs living quarters for the Catholic priest and the Lutheran minister. Both were fellow prisoners of war who had served in the army medical corps. A small group of us joined the chaplain every night after working hours for daily Mass and lively discussions. We hungered and thirsted for the truth of God's Word.

During Advent we decided to build a crèche in the chapel, according to traditional German custom. We used big pieces of cinder, which we collected for days at the coal furnaces in the barracks, to build a grotto in which the figures of the Holy Family were to be positioned. The American authorities donated plywood, lumber, paper, paint, and greenery. We built a good-sized platform for the grotto and appropriate landscaping. A large mural on the wall, painted by a talented artist in our group, provided the backdrop. After completion it looked just like a scene in the hill country outside Bethlehem. Our

work was a cooperative effort of many young people who until then were strangers, but quickly became friends.

After years of Nazi rule we were free to express our Christian beliefs again. We were grateful to our captors, who supported us in our endeavors. We had our first taste of freedom, despite the barbed wire around us. We offered our prayers for our captors, our fallen comrades, and our unfortunate brothers in Russian prison camps. On that Christmas Day in 1944, there was for us peace on earth again.

Otto Scholand
Vinton, Virginia

To Joe, in jail

My family — a husband and six children — is asleep. Each one in his or her own place . . . except for Joe. He's in jail.

My mother's heart is breaking and helpless, except for the strength that God's love gives me. And as I think about and pray for our frail, confused fifteen-year-old, I write him a letter — a letter I will not send but will hand him . . . some day.

December 19, 1972
10:45 p.m.
Christmas time

Dearest Joe,

I'm sitting here thinking about you, and with the lights of Christmas glowing through the front windows — the smell of the evergreen tree and soft, beautiful Christmas music filling the air — your place in my heart is especially empty tonight.

I pray that God keeps you from being too lonely. Someday our family will stand close together, hand in hand, hearts joined in the love that Christ teaches, and you'll know the prayer that's been in His heart all these years.

Have you talked to Christ as your friend? Do you let Him dry your tears and bind the wounds of broken friendships or heal the hurts of having cared for others? Does He hold you in His arms and teach you the sweetness of obedience? Does He smile as you take your first steps as a man? Is He calling you through the talents He placed in your mind and your sensitive, eager hands?

Will you let Him show you how to build up His world by every job you do and then let you know He will help you do everything better and better?

If I think of the Joe with the sharp sense of humor, the flashing, angry eyes, the thin, solemn son of ours sitting in a gray sheriff's office downstairs from the jail where bars confined you from "society," I fail to comprehend the thoughts of so young a boy in so strange a world.

May God sharpen your memory with compassion for every little miserable boy alone somewhere, fighting a battle deep within, and may He teach you to stretch out those sensitive hands to heal a fellow human being as your lives cross on the journey of struggle.

All my love and hope for you as your mother prompts me to say: May the Christ Child who caused the angels to sing in joy fill you this Christmas season with peace, and hold you in the folds of His love!

Merry Christmas, my dearest Joe.

Love and prayers,

Mom

Joe spent time in jail off and on, but in 1984 he changed his life. With prayers to Jesus, Mary, lots of saints, and finally holy Padre Pio, he's out of the drug world, he's married, and has two beautiful daughters. He's working twelve to fourteen hours a day to build a new business.

The consolation I had through all those years were passages from the Bible that kept showing up, filling me with hope.

"Those that sow in tears shall reap rejoicing."

Name Withheld

The Moon of the Popping Trees

My most memorable Christmas happened in 1938, my first year with the Sioux Indians at Holy Rosary Mission, Pine Ridge, South Dakota.

It was a Christmas Eve to delight the hearts of the children of the prairie. A vagrant wind leaping down from mile-high Harney Peak in the Black Hills had swept the sky clear of clouds. Myriads of stars transformed the night into jeweled splendor. From rim to rim, across the vast arch of the sky, glimmered the Milky Way, that ribbon of light woven of flaming stars. High overhead the Great Bear danced around the North Star.

A sound, sharp as a rifle shot, broke the stillness. Then came another and another, as giant cottonwoods along White Clay Creek popped open. The midnight frost was splitting their gnarled trunks. With good reason the Sioux call December "The Moon of the Popping Trees." Far away came the rhythmic yapping of a coyote serenading the heavens.

As the hour approached for Midnight Mass, the Sioux, like the shepherds of old, were hastening to come and adore. Ambrose Iron Rope galloped up on a clean-limbed pinto, the clip-clop of the hoofs ringing on the hard-packed dirt road leading to the chapel. David Crazy Thunder's weather-beaten wagon creaked out of the darkness. Hoary frost coated the withers of his sorrel team. Crazy Thunder drew up in front of the fence. He tossed the lines to his dark-eyed son, grasped the brake rigging with trembling hand, and eased his aging frame over the wheel to the ground. Old squaws wrapped in shawls bright as poinsettias entered noiselessly in moccasins decorated with bright beads. Young girls with braided hair black as the magpie's wing knelt before the crib. The shepherds of Bethlehem made no more devout or colorful a sight than the faithful Sioux crowding into the cedar-incensed house of prayer.

As the tinkling bells of Consecration announced the coming of the Prince of Peace, the Sioux bent in adoration before their newborn King, whose fingers had scooped out the weird depths of the Bad Lands.

At Communion time, *Wakan Tanka* the Great Spirit, who walks on the wings of the wind and rides the clouds for chariots, came into the hearts of His children of the prairie.

Father John M. Scott. S.J.
Omaha, Nebraska

A moment of clarity

It was Christmas Eve and I was drunk, sitting in the choir loft of St. Mary's Catholic Church. My wife, Lori, and I had been visiting my parents, and the celebrating of our family was just another opportunity for me to get smashed. I had fallen from my faith and left the Church years before. When visiting my folks, I was usually racked with guilt, and would attend Mass only because it was expected.

As the choir was warming up, and people were filing into the darkened church, I felt an inner swelling of emotion, a feeling that was altogether new for me, and my eyes were transfixed by a sanctuary light flickering before the Tabernacle. Tears began to run down my ruddied face, and I felt a longing, such a longing, to come back to God, to my Catholic faith. In a moment of brilliant clarity, I knew that God had placed me in that church to begin to be healed.

It took three years. I came back to the sacraments, Lori and I had our marriage blessed, but my drinking continued. Eventually Lori took my son Cody and left me.

I was desperate, and scared to death about all that was happening to me. And in another brief moment of brilliant clarity, I knew I was a drunk, screamed it aloud, and I called for help. The help was there. That was December 13, 1987.

Lori and Cody came back to me, and a quantum leap forward brings me to this moment. I feel such gratitude for the second chance at life that I received from God, and it all began on that Christmas Eve twelve years ago.

Dick Dawson
Traverse City, Michigan

Unexpected guests

I was driving from Akron to Buffalo on Christmas morning 1984 to visit my mother when I was engulfed by a huge blizzard. I kept my eyes glued to the red tail light in front of me, hoping the driver knew where he was going and that I would soon reach a clearing. This went on for many miles. Suddenly I realized we had left the highway, and I found myself in the town of North Kingsville. The snow was deep and the temperature around zero.

I went to a school that was housing stranded travelers. While having a cup of coffee at the school, a gentleman and his son invited me to come to their house. I was reluctant; I hoped to be able to go on to Buffalo later that day. But I went with another stranded family from Illinois. When we arrived at the house, we were welcomed by the rest of the family. Everyone began introducing themselves. There was dead silence when I said I was a Dominican sister, but only for a moment. Those kind and generous people shared their Christmas dinner with us, and entertained us with video games and pleasant conversation. I couldn't go on to Buffalo that day, and they provided overnight accommodations, too.

The daughter of the family and I stayed in touch and became friends.

This experience will live in my memory as the best Christmas present one can receive. I experienced generosity, kindness, and joy — and the Holy Spirit led me to a new friend.

Sister Denise Macko, O.P.
Akron, Ohio

My father knows me

I was happier about Dad's present than mine the Christmas of my thirteenth year. For the first time in my life, my father could see.

Early in December, surgeons removed my father's right eye to remove pressure on his left eye. The operation succeeded; Dad could then see fully through his left eye for the first time in fifteen years. The gift that God had given me, so I believed, was that my father could see me this Christmas. Before that he could touch, smell, and hear me. Somehow, at thirteen, I didn't think Dad could really know me until he could see me.

When I told Dad late that Christmas evening that I was glad he could see me, he clarified the act of knowing me. "I know you," Dad said, "through the sound of your laughter, through your sitting on my lap as I told you stories, and through knowing your hurt when you had ear trouble." My greatest gift that Christmas was learning that we "know" people and things in many ways, not through the eyes alone.

Harry Langdon
Kansas City, Missouri

The rejected child

On Christmas Day, some years ago, a middle-aged couple came to me and requested baptism for the child whom the woman was cuddling in her arms. They had traveled six hours by canoe to the town of Nova Olinda, Brazil, along the Madeira River. I was pastor of the parish of Our Lady of Nazareth. The couple were not the parents of the child. The baby had been born blind. Her parents were sickened by the thought of raising a blind child and rejected it. This story was hard to take on the day Christ was born, although the beautiful adoptive parents warmed my heart. The three of us baptized the little girl, and on her first Christmas she became a child of God and sister of Jesus Christ.

Father Joseph Glancy, T.O.R.
Loretto, Pennsylvania

The bells of Venice

Gina, Carolyn, and I, three nineteen-year-old students on vacation, arrived by train in Venice, Italy, on Christmas Eve in 1929.

From the train station we were escorted to the Grand Canal where a gondola awaited us. By stepping into it, we stepped into another world. Each lamp along the waterway wore its own halo. And the bells — those wonderful bells — large booming bells and many smaller ones, continuously calling to one another and responding in every pitch, tone, tempo, and volume, pealing out the good news.

We attended Midnight Mass at St. Mark's Basilica; we were not Catholic, and there was much of the service that we did not fully understand, but the music was superb and we easily understood the reverent adoration on the faces of those around us. I felt uplifted, transported by something that I did not comprehend, but it was joyful and comforting. I seemed to belong there.

Two weeks later, back "home" in Paris, some of what I had felt in Venice stayed with me. I wanted to understand it more fully — to know why I felt that way. I accompanied my French family to Mass each week. I read a great deal and talked to many people. By the end of the school year, I knew what I had to do. Despite opposition and disapproval of some of my relatives and friends, I must become a Catholic.

On September 18, 1931, I was baptized at St. Mary's Church in Colorado Springs, Colorado. Next Christmas will mark the sixty-third anniversary of that glorious night in Venice. It is my most memorable Christmas because it set my feet on a new path that altered my life in many ways and has been most meaningful to me.

Marguerite L. Wilgus
Longview, Texas

Too much loss

Recently I viewed an old home movie, taken at Christmas 1968, of a seven-year-old girl opening gifts. That little girl was me. What was so amazing was the fact that all seemed normal: the pretty dress, the decorated tree, the festive gifts. But nothing was normal.

Just two days earlier, the little girl's five-year-old brother, the brother she adored, had died. The months-long battle with cancer — the needles, the hair loss, the vomiting, and the pain — was over. I had lost my best friend.

Looking at that film twenty-one years later, I pinpointed the source of some of the strong mistrust I carried in my heart. In the next twenty years, I had more pieces of my spirit broken: five new siblings who never quite filled the void, rejection by my father, divorce of my parents, one failed marriage and a second struggling one, and the shocking discovery that my dad, whose love I had longed for all my life, was not my biological father at all.

After my divorce from a man who had crushed all trust I had placed in him, I rebelled. I rejected the Church and all its teachings, became agnostic, and severed my relationship with my mother, a strong Catholic. In the next four years, I had two babies, yet had never felt more isolated and depressed. I slowly went down, until April 1989, when I tried to end my life.

In the past one-and-a-half years, while in therapy, God has been pulling me toward healing. It's been an intense struggle, seemingly impossible at times, but with God, there are no impossibilities. With His guiding hand, through the intercession of Mary, I am healing my broken relationships. God has waited patiently for my complete surrender to His will in blind faith and trust.

While Christmas of 1968 gave me the beginnings of a broken spirit, this year I thank the Lord for allowing me to live for the hope of eternal peace in our Savior, Jesus Christ.

Mrs. Kim Cortino
Mission Viejo, California

Six sleds for six kids

The "year of the sleds" came when Christmas was still unbelievably magical.

We six children ranged in age from sixteen to two. With this many children and only one bathroom, every morning was chaotic at our house, but none more so than Christmas morning. Because there was no heat in the upstairs of our old Manchester home — except in the bathroom — this room became a gathering place of sorts. On this particular Christmas morning, three or four of us too young to care about privacy filled the small room with teasing and giggling.

In the kitchen, Mom was standing by the stove stirring a hug pan of oatmeal just as though this was an ordinary, everyday sort of winter's dawn.

Finally it was time. "All set?" Dad asked, as if he couldn't tell, then we all lined up on the stairsteps — shortest to tallest, silly with excitement — and the living-room doors were flung open. There on the mantle were our six stockings in graduated sizes, hung the night before but now looking so wonderfully different with lumpy shapes and colorful treats sticking out at odd angles. And there, unbelievably, standing against the wall beyond the tree, stood six shiny sleds. Six sleds in graduated sizes, all lined up just like we were!

My seven-year-old eyes could hardly take in the wonder of it all. We all squealed with delight as each of us flew to the Flexible Flyer that was just as tall as we were. For the rest of that magical morning in 1948, we all sat on our sleds on the living room floor and exchanged gifts with each other and dreamed of snow.

It was many years later that I learned that most of the sleds that we received that Christmas were not actually new. Most

were old ones that my dad had salvaged from somewhere and lovingly sanded, painted, decorated, and varnished down in a secret spot in the basement. But the eyes of this one small girl never even noticed.

Susan Howes Peowski
Mystic, Connecticut

Old times' sake

A few days before my ninth Christmas, Dad announced that I was finally old enough to attend Midnight Mass. I was all excited, and felt so grown up. I didn't get many chances to stay up late.

Snow had fallen earlier in the day, and it crunched beneath our boots as we set out. The air was sharp and crisp, and stars twinkled in the sky like diamonds on navy blue velvet. We drove right by the big church in the city, the church I was used to. Dad said we were going several miles farther, to the church in the little village where he grew up, "just for old times' sake."

St. Leo's was a picture straight out of Currier and Ives: creamy yellow, with two enormous blue spruces standing sentinel on the front lawn. Inside it was dark and mysterious. The air full of the scent of candlewax, incense, and evergreens. Candles flickered, the glow shining off every polished surface, mirroring the stars outside. I snuggled in close to Dad, feeling safe, warm, and expectant. In the front stood a crèche, the manger empty. Where was the Christ Child?

Suddenly, a deep organ blast cut through the hush. I hadn't seen the organ, and the unexpected chord made the hair stand on the nape of my neck. Somewhere behind me a women's choir announced the Savior's coming in a traditional French-Canadian carol. In my nine-year-old mind, this was the angels singing.

A solemn processional came into view, bringing with it the Bethlehem Child, who with great reverence was given His proper place in the crèche. The Mass followed, but to me it was anticlimactic. The angel choir had sung, telling one more time of a tiny baby, asleep on a rude bed of straw.

Wilfred H. Bergeron Jr.
Concord, New Hampshire

A blessing in pencil

We went broke in the winter of 1986. My husband and I had just lost a business a couple of months before and were facing a mountain of debt. We were determined to make good on our financial obligations.

We moved from a prestigious area in the city into a run-down house that looked more than one hundred years old. The children appeared to take in stride the change in our finances, but I was upset. The Christmas season that year was a mockery to me, and I hated the festive air. Christmas Eve was a quiet time for us. Our social life had plummeted to zero. I was so depressed that I hid the Christmas ornaments in the basement. I wished I could sleep the whole Christmas day away.

That midnight, the children crept quietly into our room. I was awakened by our youngest daughter, who whispered in an excited voice, "Hurry up, Mom! Open this!" I reluctantly opened a flat package wrapped in a brown paper bag. I felt my husband's arm around me as we both stared at their gift. It was a pencil drawing of our family. The children had captured our once-happy expressions.

I felt blessed by their offering. I looked at the children's beaming faces with tears in my eyes and thought, "We are a family. We lost a house but not a home. We are short of money but not of love. This is what really matters in life."

Evelina M. Mabini
Hales Corners, Wisconsin

An archbishop remembers

Three Christmas celebrations have very special memories for me. On the afternoon of Christmas Day 1952, after our family dinner, I went to our empty parish church in Sharon Hill, Pennsylvania. I was a senior in high school, and Jesus had given me the precious gift of a priestly vocation. On that Christmas I had the privilege of saying yes to that gift.

"Jesus," I thought, "You gave up all to become man and to be born in a stable so that we might be saved and might have the privilege of living with You in heaven. I am grateful for the wonderful gifts You have given me — my life, my family, my faith, and I want to offer all these gifts to Your service."

The second memory: A year after my priestly ordination, when I was a student priest in Rome, I got a telegram that my father had died on December 23. I flew home to be with my mother and reached the Philadelphia airport at midnight on Christmas Eve. The next day I celebrated three Christmas Masses in the Convent of the Holy Child Jesus in Sharon Hill. About sixty sisters, who sang Christmas hymns in beautiful polyphony, were present with my mother and grandmother for all three Masses. The decorations in the spacious convent chapel and the Christmas music certainly contrasted with my own emotions and brought back memories of past Christmases with my father and mother. Frankly, I could hardly get through the Masses, so overcome was I with emotion.

The third Christmas I remember very clearly was my first Christmas in Rome as an archbishop. After celebrating the Christmas Vigil Mass at the North American College for the students and my mother, I took my mother to the Holy Father's Midnight Mass at St. Peter's Basilica, for which I did the television commentary for fifteen nations of the English-speaking world, including the United States. The Holy Father gave my mother a special blessing as he passed her in the basilica. To see this, and to realize that I was bringing his words and indeed the story of the first Christmas to millions of people around the world, made me more grateful than ever that I had said "yes" to the call of Jesus thirty-two years earlier in Holy Spirit Church, Sharon Hill, when I knelt alone before the manger scene to thank God for the gift of himself and for His special gifts to me. His generosity continues far beyond our limited capacity to respond.

Archbishop John P. Foley
President, Pontifical Council for Social Communications
Rome

One family — white, brown, red, yellow

When I was eleven years old, we lived in Superior, Arizona, a mining community where many Canadian and Mexican workers were employed. Everyone was friendly, but the two races didn't do much socializing together.

On Christmas Eve 1959, my father went to pick up my cousin for our large family gathering. On the way, he tried to cross a normally dry creek bed located in the middle of the road. A sudden flash flood caught the car and swept it away. The people of our small town swarmed down on the creek bed in a desperate attempt to find them. They searched in the darkness in heavy rain, carrying flashlights, lamps, and shining headlights down on the water.

I remember men taking shifts and coming indoors drenched from hours of wading in the dangerous water. Some of them wore their holiday suits that they didn't even take time to change.

Everyone prayed for us, brought us food, talked to us, hugged us, or tried desperately to console us. Some of these people we had never met before. Never for one moment were we left alone. Instead of trying to celebrate Christmas without us, everyone shared in our pain and tried to comfort us in the best way they knew how. An Indian lady and her daughter came to our home, knelt down, and prayed in a chanting and beautiful way.

On the twenty-fifth in the evening my cousin's body was found. On the third day after the accident my father's body was found miles downstream. His death and the death of my

cousin had brought people in our town together, not in happiness, but in brotherly love in that Christmas season. That night the different races — white, brown, red, yellow — all were one family through love and compassion.

Gloria Jean Zepeda Gutierrez
Mesa, Arizona

Pastoral care

Five days before Christmas 1969, our home was extensively damaged by fire. All our clothing and furniture were destroyed, along with everything we had bought for Christmas for our thirteen children aged two to eighteen. Our house was unlivable. We were thankful that God had spared the family from any injury, but we were discouraged and depressed. We had no place to stay for the immediate future. No one had room for our large family, and we didn't want to be separated. Christmas looked bleak and the future looked bleaker.

Then we got a call from our pastor, Monsignor John Gordon, who offered to let us stay rent-free at an old rectory. Monsignor Gordon rounded up a volunteer crew of parishioners and put them to work cleaning and repairing the rectory. Our pastor then borrowed fifteen beds from a local child-care institution and collected blankets and clothing from parishioners. On December 23, our family moved in. We were grateful to be together in a warm house, but still we were a bit gloomy at the prospect of a not-so-merry Christmas.

On Christmas Eve, in the middle of a heavy snowstorm, two police squad cars pulled up to the rectory. Two policemen delivered boxes of presents for the family. The children were delighted, and we were in a state of shock. On Christmas, a local bakery delivered a beautiful cake, and fellow parishioners sent food.

The kindness, warmth, and love we experienced that Christmas, and during the eight months we lived at the rectory, made it seem like a palace. When our last child was born a couple of years later, we named him John Gordon Cosgriff in honor of the man responsible for that Christmas, Monsignor Gordon.

Edwina and Gene Cosgriff
Staten Island, New York

This is not a test

Seventeen years ago I was feeling sorry for myself during the holiday season. My husband and I had not been able to have children. I had no business wandering through the toy department of a department store, yet there I was.

Then a store display caught my eye. It was a Christmas tree, decorated with children's names and ages. Each ornament on the tree represented a child in need. The list was simple — one or two wishes: a doll, crayons, blocks. I chose two names and went happily on my way, delighted with the chance to shop for toys and small things. I got the holiday spirit back.

That night, the phone rang. We were in the middle of an adoption process. Our social worker called at nine p.m. to say that she had two babies who needed a home for Christmas.

I thought it was a test: If we looked after these children through the holidays, we might be approved. But the social worker continued. These were children who needed a *permanent* home by Christmas. An emergency had arisen in their foster home. After seven years on a waiting list, our names had been chosen. They would be arriving in a week.

Family, friends, and strangers helped us get ready. We didn't have a stick of baby furniture. For that matter, we didn't have a bedroom. A neighbor spent every night with my husband converting an unused sewing room into the babies' room. My sister brought one crib, a neighbor another. A teacher gave us a child's bureau. Someone else arrived with car seats. I was teaching adult basic education at night, and our Christmas party turned into a surprise baby shower. Someone I had never met knocked on our door, bringing handmade mittens.

The babies arrived twelve days before Christmas. They had

all the clothing, toys, and baby items they needed — all because others reached out to lend a helping hand. In addition to shopping for my own children (three now) every year since, I still choose the names of two children from a store Christmas tree. It keeps a wonderful memory fresh.

Ann Geisel
Greenfield, New Hampshire

The night visitor

A number of years ago, I was a patient in the hospital on Christmas Eve. Our daughters, Sandra and Mary, ages four and two, were staying with my parents. Bill, my husband, was working overtime in the post office. I was very lonely. The street lights were shining brightly and the night was very still. The snowflakes were softly falling and the earth looked like a fairyland. All was well, except for me.

There was a knock on my door and a young man entered. He was a stranger to me, tall and lanky and about twenty years old.

"I'm Jerry Hald," he told me, "from Olympia, Washington. I'm visiting in your town." He grinned, a dimple in his chin. "May I sing some Christmas carols for you?"

I nodded my head in amazement.

In a soft tenor voice, Jerry sang "Away in a Manger" and "Silent Night." As he turned to leave, I asked him, "Why did you come to see me?"

"Last Christmas Eve, I was in a hospital in Canada," he told me. "I was lonely and depressed and a stranger came to visit me. I wanted to pass it on."

Jerry left and my loneliness was gone, as I realized God had provided an angel of mercy to make my Christmas Eve a meaningful one. Every Christmas Eve, I remember Jerry and pray for him. May God bless him as he blessed me.

Sylvia Chalupsky
Burwell, Nebraska

Grief and a golden dawn

At three o'clock Christmas morning, I received a telephone call to please come home immediately.

As I hurriedly drove down over the hill into our little town, I thought this must have been the same kind of night that Jesus was born in a stable in Bethlehem so many years ago. It was a cold, clear night, and the stars were shining brightly.

As I entered my parents' home, I heard voices praying. There at my dear mother's bedside knelt our parish priest and several members of my family praying the Rosary, as Mother did faithfully and lovingly every day. Recently, she had lost her first-born son, my oldest brother, in a tragic accident. Her aged, tired, and grieving heart had failed.

At daybreak, I drove back up the hill to my home with a heavy heart. At the top of the hill I saw the most beautiful, golden sunrise that I have ever seen. I stopped in the middle of the road and stared at this glorious sight. The heaviness in my heart lifted. God had chosen to take my mother to her eternal rest on this the most wonderful day of the year — Christmas, Jesus our Savior's birthday.

Sophy Rozinsky
West Newton, Pennsylvania

The Christmas pig

Roasted pork is the traditional Christmas dish in Cuba. On Christmas Eve 1958, my grandfather and I went to the local farmer's market to buy a pig that Grandma would cook that night. My grandfather was a tall, handsome, and strong man, whose fortune consisted of his dignity and faith in God's commandments. Christmas, to him, symbolized a time for peace, love, and fellowship.

That morning, on the way back home, we pledged to repeat this outing every year. "When I grow up, Grandpa," I promised him, "I'll pick you up and we'll come to the market to buy the pig." Grandpa, a man of few words, held my hand tightly and just smiled.

A week later, Fidel Castro overthrew General Batista's government, and our family emigrated to Chicago. I grew up, married, and moved to a different state, but neither of us forgot the pledge we made to each other in 1958. Every Christmas, we reminded each other that our deal was still on. "We will, son," he'd reply. "We will, someday."

On Christmas 1982, I traveled to Chicago with my wife and children. I learned that a Latin American grocery store had recently opened near my grandfather's house. This establishment sold pigs, and I thought it was time for Grandpa and me to fulfill our pledge. This time, however, our roles were different. Grandpa was not the strong man he had been twenty-four years earlier. He now depended on me for support and security. Even though his feeble legs could not hold him for long periods of time, he was determined to meet his end of the deal. With great effort, we walked from his house to the store, two blocks away. At the store, we purchased a plump piglet that provided the best Christmas dinner I've ever tasted.

Several days later, before my family and I returned to Florida, my grandfather and I embraced and renewed our promise to do it again the following year. Unfortunately, that was to be our last hug. He died the following fall.

I'll always remember the happy moments that we spent together, shopping for the traditional Christmas-dinner pig. In memory of my grandfather, my son and I now carry on that tradition; and every Christmas Eve we look for the best pig we can find.

My grandfather's legacy reawakens in my heart and soul every year — the miracle of Christmas. Through a simple act, such as the purchase of Christmas dinner, he taught me an unforgettable lesson in love, trust, and unity.

Jordan Rivers
Miami, Florida

A collect call from Pat

Around holiday time in 1988, I was missing my oldest daughter, Pat, terribly. I worried about her health and safety. At twenty-four, she was a married woman, her husband away from the area, and her life chaotic and somewhat dangerous. Sometimes, I heard nothing from her for months at a time, and wondered where she was and what she was doing.

On Christmas Eve she called me collect. I had a fleeting vision of a phone meter somewhere racking up a huge bill, but I was thrilled to hear from her and we talked away. We chatted about our lives, her siblings and their concerns, and exchanged friendly gossip about our extended family and friends. Gradually, we slipped into talk about things that had happened over the years, funny or poignant things, but mostly the hilarious happenings that make family legends. We laughed a lot, shed a couple of tears, and then she waxed poetic over her dreams for the future: build a log cabin, start a business, and write a best-selling novel.

I told her how much I loved and missed her, and we sang "Silent Night" together. We talked for four hours.

It was the last Christmas we would ever share. Nine months later, Pat was murdered. Every year at holiday time, I treasure the memory of that lovely phone call, a most precious Christmas gift.

Jo Ann Schlicker
Wayland, New York

Of mice and Mass

My first Christmas Eve as pastor of the towns of Ridgely and Denton on the rural eastern shore of Maryland started poorly. It was unusually cold — ten degrees and a twenty-mile-a-hour wind rolling in across the flat, frozen fields and waters. I noticed this as I stood in my backyard in Ridgely and realized that I had just locked myself out of both my car and my house, less than forty-five minutes before Christmas Eve Mass was to begin over in Denton, six miles away. A neighbor came to my rescue and got me there with less than ten minutes to spare.

The sight of the people gathered in the warmth and serenity of Christmas Eve settled me considerably. Many of them were worshiping right where their ancestors had for over one hundred fifty years. Shelter from the bitter cold night lent an extra measure of intimacy to a congregation where at least half were related somehow and no newcomer remained a stranger for long. Moreover, the place was packed, as only a little country church with pews right to the walls can be. We got Mass started without incident and not intolerably late, but as I sat listening to the readings I noticed little stirrings here and there in the usually sedate and attentive congregation.

As I was preaching in the aisle, as is my custom, I thought I saw something scoot across. Three or four sentences later, I knew I did. Mice! — driven in from the fields by the intense cold, sharing the warmth of Christmas Eve with us. Somehow it doesn't come off as romantic in real life. One part of my brain kept the homily going as if (I hoped) nothing was happening. The other part kept praying, "Please, dear God, don't let anyone scream!"

At the Eucharistic Prayer, the Fountain-Gardner clan, filling the first three pews on the left, knelt with rapt attention —

not to the altar — but to the organ bench where cousin Petey was seated in intense concentration on her playing. After Mass her husband told me they were watching a mouse crawl up her knee-high leather boots as they prayed it down half a dozen times or more. Petey has a spectacular loathing of mice.

Just as I was set to distribute Communion the whole congregation went a-titter. A mouse was snuggling up in the straw with the rest of the animals in the crèche at the base of the altar. My farm-boy acolyte secured a wastebasket and swiftly dispatched the intruder into the exterior darkness.

It's not easy to get into the permanent folklore of a parish with its roots in colonial   America, but I am confident that Christmas Eve 1982 will forever be remembered at St. Elizabeth's in Denton for the Mass of the Mice.

Father Michael B. Roark
Chattanooga, Tennessee

Born anew on Christmas

Each year I spend much of my time on Christmas Day visiting shut-ins. One year I went to the infirmary of a retirement home. I visited each patient briefly, gave them a little gift, and prayed with them. Finally, I reached a mysterious little figure under a blue blanket. Apparently asleep, she was as limp as a rag doll and so tiny she might have been a child.

Emily was a delicate lady with soft white hair and fine features. Her complexion was flawless, and her face in repose was sweet and gentle.

"We have not had any response from Emily for nearly two years," the nurse whispered. "It's only a matter of time. . . ." She then told me that Emily had come from Austria in 1933 and taken a position as a nanny. The war came, her parents died, and she never returned.

The nurse was called away, but I remained for some time watching and praying for the small figure turned on her side. Her eyes were closed, but I noticed a slight movement of her lips. I moved closer. Now I could hear her softly crooning to herself: "*Guten Abend. Guten Nacht.*" It was the old German lullaby, and I finished singing it with her. "*Mit rosen bedacht.*"

The white head stirred. The blue eyes opened slowly in wonder — softened and worn in their splendor, a bit dimmed with time. She spoke to me, "My mother . . . taught me that song."

"It's lovely," I said, "and you sing it beautifully."

Emily regarded me with a shy smile. "I would like to pray now," she said. The lovely eyes appealed to me. "Help me, please." Together we recited the Hail Mary. Emily then drifted off to sleep. It was a special moment. A most beautiful and moving thing to see and be a part of.

Later, I knelt before the crib in the chapel. Here in the manger was God's Christmas gift, His holy Child. And it seemed to me on this Christmas Day He had surely given me a special gift. I walked in the glow of this gift all day.

Emily lived for another year, and we became close friends. I visited her frequently. Our conversations were never long, but for me, very enriching. It was as though she had been born anew on that Christmas Day.

Helen Curran
St. Davids, Pennsylvania

A gift for Ramona

It was time to hand out Christmas presents in our school. Father Norbert told the boys to line up on the right, the girls on the left, and to come forward to the tables to receive their gifts.

Soon a commotion started among the girls. The boys began chanting, "Ramon is a sissy, he wants a dolly."

Father came over and asked, "What is going on here?"

Rosa piped up, "Ramon keeps trying to get in line with us."

"Is that true?" Father asked the boy.

Ramon explained, "Padre, my little sister, Ramona, is at home sick. She can't get out of bed. I don't want a present for myself. I want one for her."

With a lump in his throat, Father said, "Very well. Line up here and choose a gift for Ramona."

Juanita whispered to Ramon, "I heard a teacher say that the box wrapped in plain red paper and tied with a wide green ribbon has a rag doll in it with some extra clothes."

"Thanks for the tip. I'll take it," said Ramon.

Father gave the package to the eight-year-old and said, "Now, Ramon, step over here and choose a gift for yourself."

Ramon quickly took a ball and said, "Thank you, Padre, for the nice Christmas party."

Sister Marian Massart, O.P.
Racine, Wisconsin

Capturing water

Christmas is the hardest time to be the parent of an autistic child. We expect special days to elicit wide-eyed wonder and great expectations of joys to come, but autism robs its victims of reality as well as the hope for joy. Yet I still hoped that Michael's fifth Christmas would be different, that he'd "notice." I faced the holiday with a mixture of fear and hope, fear that for Michael there would be no Christmas joy, but hope that for just this once he wouldn't be left out.

Michael enjoyed sunshine, wind, fluttering leaves, and sea gulls. But most of all he loved water, running water. He would spend hours in our garden patiently trying to capture the stream of water that ran down from an overhead hose placed there for his amusement.

Finally Christmas arrived and Santa had spared no expense. Our tree was the prettiest ever, a ceiling-to-floor display of lights and tinsel. I couldn't wait for Michael to notice his toys. Slowly he made his way toward the gifts, hesitating momentarily, then without even a downward glance he proceeded to the flashing tree. My heart sank. He hadn't even noticed his presents.

Suddenly the house was filled with Michael's laughter as his hand shot forward grabbing a long strip of tinsel. Michael had finally captured water! His joy knew no bounds.

That was when I understood that joy cannot be bought, not for ourselves or for others. Joy is truly a gift, freely given, and Michael had not been left out. The joy brought into our world by another child long ago had extended itself down through the ages from Mary's child to mine.

Marilyn Paterson, S.F.O.
Bentonville, Arkansas

Single, homeless, pregnant

I was cold, lonely, not knowing God, trying to make sense of my miserable life. I had already decided that abortion was not an option, but I never dreamed how difficult the choice for life would be. Crying, I came upon a Nativity scene in front of one of the local churches and sat down in the snow. Looking at the statue of Mary, I said, "You too, huh?" I knew Mary and I were very different, but I could see the similarities too.

I sat there through the night, at times feelings sorry for myself, at other times feeling sorry for Mary, who was also young, pregnant, and homeless. As daybreak came, a light snow began to fall, and I felt a sense of warmth, a peace, and a confidence that everything would be OK.

Things *were* OK. I lived on the streets throughout the winter, but managed to rent a small furnished apartment before the birth of my child. I formed solid relationships with helpful people, finished high school, and was able to provide a modest living for myself and my daughter.

In 1982, both my daughter and I shared a tremendous conversion experience and became active members of the Church. We share a strong devotion to Our Lady, too. This conversion began on Christmas Eve 1962, when Jesus' gift of faith, hope, and love was planted in my heart while waiting with His mother for His birth. Each year at Advent, I

put up a manger and await the birth of Jesus, and on Christmas Eve, relive the memory of that first Christmas Eve vigil with the virgin in 1962.

This is my story, and this was my best Christmas.

Eileen O'Grady
North Adams, Massachusetts

A little boy's love

I recall a Christmas during the war years. Our little boy, Dickie, was almost three. It was nearly impossible to buy toys, yet we tried to get him what he wanted — namely, a farm set. Our son wanted the farm set because he loved to go to his uncle's farm to see the neat fences and pens for the cows, horses, pigs, and chickens. We found some toy animals, fences, and a barn. My husband made a tractor with big wheels all painted red and black.

Christmas morning arrived and Dickie was so thrilled with his farm that even the Christmas tree took second place. He looked at the tree, but was soon setting up his farm. After playing with it for a while he wandered over to the Nativity scene. We had it set up on a table. He looked at it in wonder and asked about the shepherds and the sheep. He went back to his farm and played quietly for some time. After a while he came to me clutching some tiny lambs, a calf, and a few chickens in his little hands. "I want Baby Jesus to have some of my animals," he said. Together, we went and placed them in the Nativity scene. Later when I put away the Christmas decorations, I asked him if he wanted his animals back. He said, "No, I gave them to Baby Jesus."

Even though we can well afford an expensive Nativity set today, I still set up the little old one, with a small wooden hut and figures made of plaster, scarred and peeling. I still have them among the figures and I place them around the crib. It brings back memories of a little boy's love at Christmas time.

Esther Corrigan
Amherst, Wisconsin

The Christmas bison

Several years ago, I went to Midnight Mass in West Yellowstone, Montana, a town sixteen miles from my home in Island Park, Idaho, and at the west edge of Yellowstone National Park. After Mass, I skied over the town's snow-packed streets to a trail into the park that ends at the beautiful Madison River. I glided beside the river for a half-mile and stopped in a frozen meadow. The world was silent and the sky replete with stars. I felt the hope-filled solitude I imagine the Holy Family felt the moment Jesus came into the world.

Suddenly, a sound came from the trees that edged the meadow, and a huge dark form walk toward me. It snorted like a curious pig, and I knew it was a bison. I stood still, trying to decide if I should ski away, but the bison changed direction and looked as if he would ignore me and go to the river.

Then, just as he was passing, he turned and came right up to me. I felt no panic or fear as he rubbed his head along the sleeve of my jacket. When his head made contact with me, I felt as if a friend was greeting me with kindness. Then he turned and went back along his way to the river.

As I watched him make his way through the snow, in my mind's eye, I saw the baby Jesus in Mary's arms, reaching for the bison and chuckling. This magnificent creature was indeed an awesome gift from God the Creator, as were the snow and stars and river. The encounter was a Christmas gift from God.

Elizabeth Laden
Hardin, Montana

The makeshift tree

During the winter of 1978, we moved to the country with my mother's third husband. It was one of the coldest winters in Louisiana, and we were at the poorest point I can remember. My mom's husband had a drinking problem and was gone for weeks at a time.

During Christmas that year, we couldn't even buy food, so I knew we could never afford a Christmas tree or presents. On Christmas Eve, my mom had to go to Mississippi to pick up her husband, so I was left with my younger brother to tend to. I was twelve.

We were watching a Christmas show and eating cold biscuits for supper when my little brother asked when were we putting up our Christmas tree. I looked around and tried very hard not to cry. I was very afraid of the woods where we lived.

I waited until my brother fell asleep, then crept down into the woods to find a tree. I didn't realize how difficult cutting down a tree would be. So after nearly freezing to death, I started back to the trailer empty-handed.

Just then I noticed a little evergreen bush. Actually, it was more like a tumbleweed on a stem, but I cut it down and carried it inside. I put it in our butter churn and stuffed old newspaper around it to make it stand straight.

Then I dug around in the closet for the only strand of lights we had. I wrapped them around and around the tree. I then cut out a haphazard cardboard star and covered it in aluminum foil. I placed it on the top of the tree and used bobby pins to hold it.

I stepped back and looked at my handiwork. I have to admit it looked a little funny, but it was the most beautiful tree I had ever seen.

On Christmas morning, my little brother woke me up shouting, "Santa Claus left us a tree for Christmas!" I hugged him tight and, finally, I did cry.

Dawn R. Morvan
Deridder, Louisiana

Three Masses in Paris

Christmas Eve 1946, and I was three thousand miles from home — a single, twenty-five-year-old working girl, in Paris on a one-year Civil Service assignment. France was slowly recovering from five years of Nazi occupation. The summer of 1946 in France was the coldest summer recorded in over seventy years: the food crops had failed. There were no potatoes, no rice. The average Parisian was still suffering great deprivation and struggled to survive each day.

Paris' St. Roch's Catholic Church is only two blocks from the hotel the United States War Department had provided for the American secretaries to be billeted. St. Roch is a huge, old stone parish church, famous for its organ.

Midnight Mass featured fifty five- and six-year-olds in white outfits singing off-key, with the pure innocence and enthusiasm of young children. My understanding of spoken French was minimal, but I could not mistake the love and warmth with which the families embraced their children and friends following this midnight celebration.

In no hurry to leave and walk back alone to my cold hotel room, I lingered in the glow of the congregation. Then I realized a priest had started a second Mass at a side alter, so I joined the thirty-plus people participating. The main part of the church was darker now. The atmosphere grew quieter and more spiritual. It was consoling to be part of our "own" special Eucharist. I was still reluctant to leave the church once this second Mass ended. But wait, there was a "third" Mass. Now the group that gathered before the altar numbered no more than nine. This was the most vibrant and rewarding sacrifice of the three.

I imagined that we were the shepherds at the manger,

adoring Divine Love, while the rest of the folks of Bethlehem were busy with other activities (sleeping). Those few of us all silently shared the best gift Christmas could offer — the reality and love of the Divine Son. Mass ended.

Finally, I could walk back to the hotel, no longer alone, as a quiet peace and joy filled my whole being.

C. A. Taylor
McLean, Virginia

Collapsible Christmas

I'll always remember a rather humorous event that happened one Christmas when I was about twenty years old.

My brothers and sisters and I, my parents and my grandfather all expectantly gathered around the table to enjoy the sumptuous feast that my mother had begun cooking before dawn. I can still picture the kitchen table laden with platters of delicious food, all the plates and silver, napkins and glasses laid out in perfect symmetry. The centerpiece was a huge ham. Everyone happily chatted as we loaded our plates.

Suddenly, our old, worn table decided that it had supported just one feast too many. It unceremoniously collapsed. Plates, glasses, and food were dumped in an ugly heap on the floor.

I never forget the look of incredulous horror on my poor mother's face as she took in the chaos at our feet, and my eighty-eight-year-old grandfather's look of confusion and astonishment.

Happily, most of the ham was salvaged and my dad and brothers braced the table sufficiently so that we could use it again. However, we had a much simpler version of the intended menu — namely, ham sandwiches. We occasionally recall the story with much enjoyment, but I don't think my mother will ever think it as funny as the rest of us do.

Patricia Price
Lebanon, Pennsylvania

Coming home

After college in the early '60s, I entered a convent in the midwest. After only four months there, I was abruptly told to leave and was handed a train ticket for a city near my home. I was shocked and deeply hurt. I felt that God had rejected me. Soon I left the Church, and I was away from it for six lonely, stark years.

During those years, as I see them now, God was always present in my life. This was most often evident through the people He placed in my path. One eighty-five-year-old doctor refused to allow me to believe that I was an agnostic. A woman came into my life and began to tell me about Jesus, as if I had never heard of Him. She brought me back to prayer.

As time passed, I began to hunger for the Eucharist. I began to attend charismatic prayer meetings. The hunger grew and grew. Finally, in God's time, I overcame the last of the obstacles keeping me back. I confessed my sins. I have never felt such joy as I felt that night — the night before Christmas Eve. That Christmas I came "home" in the deepest sense of the word. I received Jesus for the first time in years. Quiet peace dwelt within me. With God's grace, I have stayed home in the Lord!

Mary Runk
East Greenbush, New York

Stranded

Joseph and Mary found no room in the inn. On this Christmas Eve, hundreds of Christmas travelers were similarly without shelter in the town of North East, Pennsylvania, when a tremendous lake-effect snowstorm closed Interstate 90 at the New York State line.

The Red Cross opened a shelter in one of the public schools and called on the assistance of the fire department, of which I was chaplain. We set up cots and rescued travelers whose cars became trapped on the secondary roads. The snow continued to fall all day, and more travelers came. The Red Cross provided meals, while members of the fire department did what they could to help cheer up everyone.

At nightfall on Christmas Eve, a local minister and I conducted a service of songs and Scriptures. There was something special in the air as the stranded travelers sang "O Come All Ye Faithful" and "Away in a Manger" that night. One of the firemen dressed as Santa for the children.

At midnight, I celebrated Mass in the school library for those who were Catholic. Under the circumstances, it was a simple Mass without choir, manger, or decorations. Yet, it was a very special Mass. Those stranded travelers in North East, away from home, with few of their belongings, and no room in the inn, like Joseph and Mary, had nonetheless discovered joy in one another and in worshiping the Lord on the Day of His Birth.

Father Peter E. Sousa, C.SS.R.
Concord, North Carolina

Christmas —
after seven years

When I was nine years old, my nineteen-year-old brother, Les, was killed in a car accident. It was December 23, two days before Christmas. That was a sad and lonely Christmas, and every year it became a reminder that one of us was missing, never to return again. The grief continued and took such a hard toll on Mom and Dad that even by the next season we were not up to celebrating Christmas.

As the years went by, the same thing happened again and again: no more Christmas, no more celebration. The season of birth became the season of pain and loss.

I can remember my friends talking about "their" Christmas tree, making plans for dinner and what Mass they would be attending. I was ashamed to tell them that I no longer had a Christmas … not since Les' death.

Seven years later, I had met a young, handsome, and kind nineteen-year-old boy named Chris, who was in his first year of college. Chris was also a Catholic. As the holiday season rolled around, Chris began to ask about our plans and sought hints of gifts that I might want or use. Embarrassed and tearful, I told him about that tragic day years ago and how we still had no celebration at Christmas.

Chris seemed to understand, and his kindness and strength comforted me. But I was totally unprepared for what he did. A few days before Christmas, Chris showed up at the door with gifts — presents brightly wrapped for everyone!

At first Dad seemed upset, then gradually calmed down,

as we all laughingly sat on the floor and opened our gifts. But all of a sudden, Dad jumped up, threw on his coat, and rushed out the door, letting it slam behind him. We had pushed him too far, we thought. As the minutes ticked by, we sat silently in tears.

"It doesn't mean we don't miss you, Les," I prayed. "It doesn't mean that we don't love you. We just wanted to live again, to celebrate, to be a family once more."

A while later the door flew open and in came Dad with a Christmas tree under one arm and presents under the other. He plopped the tree in the middle of the table and said, "Merry Christmas, Chris! Merry Christmas, everyone!"

We all stood and hugged and cried as we celebrated our first Christmas in seven years.

The magic of that night has continued. Chris later became my husband.

That Christmas of long ago was a new beginning, just as Jesus had promised.

Pam Barber Diulio
Monroe, Michigan

Mass for the Dead

On Christmas Eve 1950, I was a young sailor, nineteen years old, on a Navy LST in Hungnam Harbor, Korea. We had pulled off of the beach at Hungnam loaded with Army and Marine troops as the Navy ships and airplanes kept the Chinese army at bay. These were the people who had fought and survived Ch'osan Reservoir, as well as the bitter cold. All of the ships were overloaded, not only with our troops but also with North Korean civilians who wanted to escape south.

The cold was bitter on the top deck of the LST. Snow fell, and the wind and the sea were heavy. But the Marines had with them a beautiful gift from God, a Catholic chaplain. They shared their gift with the rest of us.

Before the Mass at noon Christmas day, Father heard confessions in a forward gun mount for five hours.

In the pitching of the rough sea, a tank on the tank deck broke its mooring. Two young sailors were crushed to death against the bulkhead by the tank. Only an hour before they had stood in Father's confession line. The Mass we had that Christmas Day became the Mass for the Dead — and we held a burial at sea.

Instead of "Peace on Earth, good-will toward men," we heard the long, sad notes of the Marine Corp bugler blowing taps. And the words of the priest — that the seas will give up their dead — rang true, because "God so loved the world that he gave his only Son, that whoever believes in him should not perish but have eternal life"!

God's Christmas gift to us that day was a priest who himself was later to die in that forgotten war.

Milt V. Mann
Nashville, Tennessee

Irish blessing

I got terribly homesick my first Christmas in America. In Ireland Christmas is a great family affair, and I had no family in the United States. I realized that I would feel a lot better if I stopped thinking about myself and did something for someone else.

A friend invited me to go to a Franciscan Third Order meeting. At the meeting they asked people to volunteer to serve Christmas dinner to the poor at the Christian Action Center near Broadway in Manhattan and hand out gifts afterwards. I had expected the gifts to be more attractive than the bars of soap, toothbrushes, and similar items that I helped to wrap. But the people loved them. I saw a man cry as he exclaimed: "No one ever gave me a Christmas gift before." And another said, "I can't remember when I last received a gift."

It made me realize that my memories of Christmases past are also a gift. Instead of being sorry that I cannot relive them, I ought to be grateful that the memories are still there. I met a whole lot of grateful people that cold, bleak Christmas Day in the little room off Broadway, and they shared their joy with me and they showed me how to be grateful for all the things that I have.

Catherine Lloyd
Newport, Rhode Island

Little Thomas

About five p.m. on Christmas Eve, I went into labor. Our doctor had told us that the baby could not survive because I had been exposed to German measles. Our son died early Christmas morning, an hour after his birth. This was all the more painful because the year before we had lost a baby girl the day she was born. I went home the next day for a quiet and tearful Christmas.

Then, on December twenty-eighth, everything changed.

My husband answered the telephone. As he listened, he slowly slid down the wall and wound up, open-mouthed, sitting on the floor. He hung up, smiled, and said, "We can pick up our baby tomorrow. That was St. Vincent de Paul Orphanage. They have a little three-week-old who needs a mother and father." I was stunned.

We were so excited we rushed to get a blanket and some clothes, as we had bought nothing for our baby. Both of us realized then that we didn't know if we were adopting a boy or a girl. My husband had forgotten to ask.

It was a boy. We went to St. Vincent's the next morning and were led to the nursery. Little Thomas was placed in our arms. Tom is in college now, still our Christmas joy who came to us like a miracle at a time of loss and grief.

Anne Markus
St. Petersburg, Florida

Street woman in Bombay

Christmas in India! Though we were warned of India's great poverty, we still were not prepared for the number of the cold and homeless in the streets. Guides informed us that the government discourages donating to beggars, thus promoting the profession. Indeed, we precipitated a touchy situation when we paid to photograph a gaunt boy holding a cavernous-eyed, crippled child in his arms, one thin hand held out for alms. Immediately, an angry group of women and children descended upon him and us, attacking him and begging rupees. In response to a man's sharp reprimand, they dispersed.

We were determined to avoid any further confrontation. On Christmas Eve a lone woman, shivering in rags, reached out for help. We turned aside.

My memory of her kept me from a peaceful sleep in my comfortable bed that night in the majestic Taj Mahal Hotel. In joyful participation at Christmas Mass with Christian Indians the next morning, I tried to compensate for my neglect of the previous evening by a generous offering. But no amount of contributions to the poor since can obliterate the image of that forlorn woman on the dimly lit street corner in Bombay on Christmas Eve.

Phyllis M. Candee
San Jose, California

Becoming aware

In 1954, I was four years old, living with my family on Chicago's south side. My mother had taken my two older brothers and me shopping. My memory begins just as we got off the bus.

"Hold on to me now," my mother admonished. I was very tiny for four, but also very determined. I gripped some portion of her coat tenaciously.

Snow fell lightly. I stuck out my tongue and the snowflakes stuck and melted, feeling cool and fresh. Then, life and all its sights and sounds hit me. The street lights everywhere had been turned into candy canes, with boughs of evergreen garlanded around them. From every lantern a Santa, reindeer, or snowman beamed down. People of all shapes and sizes were talking, bustling, carrying stacks of mysterious packages. Presents, I thought! All the store windows were gaily decorated and Christmas carols streamed from the shops into the street. I felt a secret joy that made me skip.

At the end of the block, my mother said, "We'll make a visit."

We turned down the next street, and everything was suddenly quiet. The snow sparkled as it fell, transforming the world into a fairy palace.

We stopped in front of a huge building. Its massive wooden doors formed an arch and above the arch was a cross like the one in our house, where my sister and I said our prayers. This was St. Bernard's, our parish church, and as we went in, I could see that it was empty. I could hear our footsteps echo around us. Along the side wall, vigil lights flickered. The sanctuary was lighted, but otherwise all was dark and silent.

My mother, my brothers, and I knelt, but soon I sat back in the pew to look around. I gazed for a while at the angels keeping watch over the altar, but my eyes were drawn to the figure of Jesus, one hand over his heart, the other stretched out toward me. I nodded and smiled, feeling very happy.

There, my memory ends. I don't even remember going home. Yet this small scrap of memory is filled with meaning for me. It was my first semblance of awareness: awareness of nature — the beauty that surrounds us every day; awareness of people — their spirit and uniqueness; awareness of the inner spirit — the soul that needs to be continually nurtured; awareness of life. This small memory, sparking so much happiness and peace, is perhaps my soul's greatest gift to me.

Maureen Dunne
Schaumburg, Illinois

Grandma Noonan

Christmas never officially began at our house until Grandma Noonan came home for the holidays. She would arrive loaded down with shopping bags and bundles. Grandma always knew each child's heart's desire and saw to it that the special present was under the tree on Christmas.

During the war, my grandmother had moved to upstate New York to work as a nurse. Before Christmas 1943, she wrote saying she didn't think she would be able to come home for Christmas. She was having trouble finding someone to relieve her because of the wartime shortage of nurses.

Christmas without my grandmother? I was crushed.

On Christmas Eve I must have looked out the window a hundred times for a glimpse of the familiar taxi. I watched the streetlights come on and fancied I saw the Christmas Star. In my heart I made a very special wish that the star that had guided the shepherds and wise men to the baby Jesus would lead Grandma home for Christmas.

I dozed off only to be awakened by the doorbell. I flew to the door and there she was. Grandma Noonan had come home for Christmas after all.

I can't remember anything else about that Christmas. However, it remains the most special Christmas of my childhood. God had heard a little child's Christmas wish and granted it. I also cherish the memory of Grandma Noonan. She gave me many beautiful gifts. The most wonderful gift of all was her unconditional love. She thought all of her grandchildren were the brightest, prettiest, most remarkable children in the world.

Mary Borrelli
Tonawanda, New York

The shepherd's visit

The Christmas I remember best came in 1931 when I was five years old. My mother, at the young age of twenty-four, was in the state hospital with advanced Alzheimer's disease. Daddy was raising four small children. We were very poor, as was everyone in the small farming community where we lived.

Three days before Christmas, the wind outside was howling and blowing bitter cold after a month of snows. It was beginning to get dark when a shepherd knocked on our door and asked if he could pasture his sheep on our stubbled field of alfalfa. Daddy helped him with his sheep, then invited him for supper. Afterwards the man went back to his flock. Daddy called a family conference to see if he should go and bring the man in out of the cold to sleep on our living room floor. We children begrudged another mouth sharing what little food we had, but Daddy saw things in a different light. Daddy won out — a majority of one — and waded through the snow and brought the shepherd back. They talked long into the night. The shepherd stayed for two days, then moved his sheep on and we never saw him again.

When we folded the pallet blankets, we found a note of thanks, a five dollar bill for Daddy and four half-dollars for us children. Daddy took us to town for our first Christmas shopping spree.

Now, at each passing Christmas, I become more certain the shepherd was surely sent from Christ. Perhaps he was Christ.

Mrs. Bonnie Blunk
Grand Junction, Colorado

How Melissa saved Christmas

I have gone through sixty-one abundant and joyous Christmases. However, the one I recall with heartfelt appreciation was the Christmas twelve years ago — after my husband lost his well-paying job. We had eight children to support and a luxurious home to maintain. We immediately put our six-bedroom home up for sale. The timing was bad. Jobs were scarce, and houses weren't selling. It would be almost a year before my husband found a job in his area of competence.

In the interim we had to sell most of our possessions. Our beautiful boat was the first to go, then entire roomsful of exquisite antique furniture disappeared. It was embarrassing for the children when their many friends came to visit. It was kind of a "now you see it, now you don't" lifestyle. Throughout the ordeal I tried to maintain a cheerful disposition. After all, Jesus was sitting on my shoulder whispering sweet encouragement into my receptive ears. "Count your blessings." "Don't worry about tomorrow — today's troubles are enough." "The crown of life is yours if you faint not." I "fainted not" until we lost the roof over our heads and moved into a house we named the "Quonset hut."

We moved three days before Christmas. And we could not provide Christmas presents for a population of ten.

My daughter Melissa was a senior at Bennett High and worked part-time at Arby's to save money for college. After a year of hard work, plus buying her own books and clothes,

her savings climbed to one hundred eighty four dollars. She asked me to drive her to the bank so she could take a little money out to buy a gift for her best friend. While I waited in the car, gloom and depression enveloped me. I was morose because I yearned to be the one who had money to draw out for Christmas. Jesus hadn't abandoned me, but I wasn't listening to His encouraging words. Melissa slipped into the seat beside me. My heart was so heavy by now, my body could scarcely hold up under it. Melissa opened my hand and slipped most of her savings into it. She said "Mom, Merry Christmas." I couldn't speak at first because I had a lump in my throat. The tears that gently flowed down my cheeks as I drove home told her how much I loved her.

Margaret Windle
Marion, Indiana

"Venite Adoremus" — from Rome

I was a seminarian studying in Rome, spending my first Christmas outside the United States. As the holidays approached, I began to feel the truth of the old saying that home is a place one leaves with his feet, but never with one's heart. No matter how hard I tried to concentrate on other things, I really started to miss my family and homeland. And with the lines of communication so limited — telephone calls were expensive and the mail was delayed by local strikes — I began to wonder how it would even be possible to give my family something memorable that Christmas.

But a few days before Christmas, our community was asked to supply servers for the midnight Mass celebrated by Pope John Paul II at St. Peter's Basilica. I would be on worldwide television. I got anxious. Would I look OK? What if I made a mistake? How would I greet the Pope? Rehearsals helped to reduce these fears, and prayer set them into perspective. I had managed to contact my parents on Christmas Eve with a quick phone call, telling them the good news. They promised to watch.

Meeting the Holy Father in person and assisting at his prayerful celebration of the Mass left an impression upon me that I find hard to describe and difficult to forget. But one moment struck me in particular. During the final procession, we followed the Pope to the Christmas crib, where he placed the Christ Child in the manger. I was carrying a candle behind the Pope. I saw the TV cameras. People all

over the world were part of this event. Strains of *"Adeste Fidelis"* bounded off the ornate ceiling and walls decorated by the likes of Bernini and Michelangelo. The song echoed to the depths of the crypt below, hallowed by the tombs of saints. Clerics and religious, men and women from various countries and ways of life, all joined in the refrain *"Venite Adoremus!"* I wasn't nervous any more and I, too, joined in the verse of the only Latin song I knew by heart.

At that moment, I felt at one with my family, not just the one watching me hundreds of miles overseas, but with my larger family, the Church. All of us, great and small, were coming together in Christ, resounding the praises of God! This new family brought me peace and consolation at a troubled time.

Frank Giuffre
Milwaukee, Wisconsin

Answered prayers

In 1961, my husband left me and our two-year-old daughter, Nancy. I tried to make ends meet, but jobs were scarce — especially for girls who were high-school dropouts. My mother-in-law offered to keep Nancy until I got on my feet. As much as I hated being separated from my baby, I felt that I had no choice.

Being jobless, I was also soon homeless. Indiana can be very cold in the winter. Sometimes I would sleep in someone's car, sometimes I would wrap myself in newspapers and go anywhere I could find a place to get out of the wind. I walked the streets of my hometown and felt so alone.

Christmas night was the worst. Nothing was open for business. I knew I would have to walk around until the morning of the twenty-sixth before I could find a place to get warm. I walked by homes and watched families laughing, talking, and loving one another. I called my mother-in-law to ask if I could be with my daughter just for Christmas. No one answered. I walked by their house; it was dark. I walked, prayed, and cried all night. I asked God to show me how to get my life in order.

There was no sudden miracle, but within two weeks I had a job and a room. The job barely paid my room rent, with a few dollars left over. I saved every cent I could. By the summer of 1963 I had my little girl back with me. I found my husband, and tried to get our marriage back together. He would stay for a few days, then leave for weeks. By November I was pregnant, and he was gone again. Thanksgiving went by and I didn't see my husband. It was just a couple of days before Christmas. My husband had my car, and I didn't know how to reach him.

The money I earned took care of the necessities, but there was none left for extras. I looked in my purse: fifteen dollars. I knelt by my bed and asked God to help me give my daughter a nice Christmas. Then I dressed Nancy up warmly, and we went trudging through the snow to the nearest shopping center.

I bought her a cup of hot chocolate and sat her where I could shop and watch her at the same time. That fifteen dollars went farther than I ever dreamed possible. There were bargains galore! I bought a doll, a tea set, and books. I even bought bright-colored lights and a tree.

The snow was beautiful, and the walk home was fun. We sang Christmas carols. We played in the snow. When we got home we decorated the tree with lights and homemade ornaments. We listened to Christmas music and had cinnamon toast and tea. We laughed, played, and prayed together.

Nancy is thirty-three now, and I have more children and grandchildren. There have been many Christmases since, but none as special as the one we shared years ago.

Kay Zinn
Lorena, Texas

A Serbian Saul

I will never forget Christmas 1991. That was when I became a Catholic — against impossible odds!

I come from Serbian ancestry, raised in a Serbian home: hatred for Catholics, particularly Croatian Catholics, was deeply ingrained in me. I was a very active and committed member of a fundamentalist and charismatic church. I preached and taught at every opportunity that the Catholic Church was the biggest, most powerful, and most dangerous anti-Christian cult of all. I was a rising leader in the church. I was even becoming successful at bringing some people out of the Catholic Church. Anti-Catholic agitation was my strongest passion. The possibility of my ever becoming Catholic was unthinkable.

Yet at Christmas 1991, I found myself in a Catholic church, deep in prayer, with tears rolling down my cheeks, earnestly praying that my Serbian brothers would stop killing my Croatian brothers and sisters. I am now totally, completely and devoutly a Roman Catholic. All the energy and talent that had been directed against the Church, I am now, by the grace of God, using to build and strengthen His Church and the Faith.

Prayer caused this modern-day Saul to be transformed into a Paul. It was the deep, consistent, unwavering faithful prayers of those that I had offended so deeply that enabled all this to happen.

The Christmas gifts we give and receive can be reminders of the many and plentiful and tremendous gifts that He wants so much to bestow on us, if only we will receive them.

David Mandarich Spencer
San Bernardino, California

Sober

My most memorable Christmas was in 1989. After spending twelve months in a drug-treatment facility, I was discharged December 22. For the first time in over ten years, I spent Christmas Eve with my family and friends. And for the first time in ten years, I went to Midnight Mass, spending Christmas Eve in a beautiful church instead of in a cheap hotel room sharing drugs and "war stories" with other drug addicts.

As the choir and congregation began to sing the old, and very beautiful, Christmas songs and hymns, I broke into tears. Tears of gratitude for being "clean," of joy, and, yes, of sadness, for all the lost years and wasted Christmases.

For the first Christmas in ten years, I was able to join in the Christian community and raise my voice and prayers to God instead of walking the streets seeking and using drugs.

For the first Christmas in ten years, I was able to receive the Body and Blood of Jesus Christ instead of a needle in my arm and the sickening rush that comes from doing another "hit."

For the first Christmas in ten years, I was able to actually sit upright and listen to the words of the priest instead of being sprawled out on a hotel-room bed, covered with vomit and blood. For the first Christmas in ten years, the words "May Peace be with you" meant just that — a true and inner peace — the kind of peace that warms the soul and makes one right with God.

And finally, for the first Christmas in ten years, I was surrounded by people who loved me and cared about me. For the first Christmas in ten years, I was part of the human race.

Ronald S. Endersby
White City, Oregon

The missing doll

During the Depression we lived on a farm in northern Idaho. The Christmas I was eight, we were nestled away in the snow-covered forest. The woodlands provided fuel and an elegant tree for the holiday season, but my parents had only thirty-five dollars to see us through the winter months. We children anticipated Christmas and the surprises of Christmas morning with unbounded joy. Our mother disappeared upstairs for long hours. Sometimes I think she was weeping.

A few weeks before Christmas, a favorite homemade rag doll named Cinderella disappeared. Something inside me said, "Don't inquire!" She had become really dirty and torn, but I loved her.

Christmas morning arrived, and we children rushed to the tree with the usual excitement. Waiting for me under the branches was a colorful clown doll, the same size as the lost Cinderella. The clown was decorated with bright bits and pieces of cloth scraps left over from sewing projects. It was beautiful, but I felt both joy and sadness. By some intuition, I knew that my mother had made this doll from Cinderella, using what she had on hand. I let out a shriek of delight and snuggled the little clown to my heart. I understood that it was a genuine gift of love, and that is the true happiness of Christmas.

Years later, my mother brought up the fact that she had made the clown from my old rag doll. "You didn't know the difference," she commented, "and liked the clown doll." I smiled to myself because I knew what she had done. I loved and remembered the gift all my life.

Cassie Eugenia Tartoué
Moscow, Idaho

Light of the world

One of the most heart-warming of Christmas experiences for us Catholics is attendance at Midnight Mass. It had been my pleasure for many years to decorate the altars in our church and to prepare the Bethlehem scene in such a way that the congregation could feast their eyes on flowers, candelabra, statues and lighted trees, and revel in the exterior beauty of this most beloved feast.

On this particular Christmas I felt that I had outdone myself in making the sanctuary attractive. The church was filled to overflowing. The ushers were setting up extra chairs to accommodate the latecomers. All was in readiness except to ring the bells and turn on the lights. The bells were rung; the lights were turned on. The people rose to greet the entering procession. The priest and his retinue moved toward the altar when, suddenly, all the lights went off! Nothing was visible except the flicker of candles casting tree shadows on the walls.

I was devastated. "After so much preparation," I thought, "how could this happen? No one can see anything." But the pastor commented on the appropriateness of celebrating the birth of Christ in darkness, for this is how He really came. The congregation caught the spirit. A reverence pervaded the church such as I had not felt on previous Christmases.

Toward the end of the Mass, the lights went on as suddenly as they had failed. A gasp of delight rippled through the rows of assembled people. Smiles played on their faces. They seemed to be saying, "He has come. The Light of the World is here."

Sister Diane Kotowski
Rice Lake, Wisconsin

When I met Christ

It was Christmas Eve — twenty minutes before midnight, to be exact. The stockings were hung by the chimney with care, the tree was trimmed, the presents were wrapped and hidden away. My family was walking to midnight Mass at St. Lawrence Church, two blocks away.

We crunched through the snow on a crisp, clear night, full of Christmas joy. Suddenly out of the darkness a young man appeared. He walked up to me and uttered a few words in Spanish. By the light of the street lamp I could see that he was dressed in skin-tight jeans and a shabby suit coat with an upturned collar suitable for summer but not for that frigid night. He wore no hat or gloves. In English and with gestures I told him that I did not understand him. Again he spoke in Spanish and again, a bit impatiently perhaps, I said I could not understand what he was trying to tell me. He shrugged, shoved his hands in his coat pockets and ambled off.

Quickly we continued on to church so as not to be late for Mass. At the door I stopped; I could not go in. An inner voice was speaking to me. "What have you done? That man was cold and probably hungry and you let him go on. You have two warm coats. You could at least have given him one."

I left my family in church and rushed back, but the stranger was gone. "He couldn't have gone very far," I thought. I got into my car, and for about fifteen minutes I cruised the streets in the general direction he had gone. I never saw him again.

That was forty years ago, and on every Christmas Eve since I have thought with sadness and regret of the night

when I met Christ, naked and hungry, and because I was so engrossed in my own joy and merriment I failed to recognize Him and to clothe and feed Him on His birthday.

Emile J. Monfils
Hurtsboro, Alabama

A home by the river

Though I am seventy-seven years old, I vividly remember a Christmas that began in a Baltimore, Maryland, orphanage when I was eight years old.

Three days before Christmas a woman in the orphanage came to me and said, "There is a nice lady in the parlor who would like to talk to you and I want you to be very polite to her." The unforgettable part of my conversation was when that lady in the parlor asked me, "How would you like to have your very own home on a farm with horses, cows, pigs, chickens, ducks, and geese — all by a river where you can go swimming and fishing?" I politely responded that I would like it. I realized that a whole new world was being offered to me.

The day before Christmas, at dusk, I found myself riding in a horse-drawn buggy with the lady and her husband. "It will be a long trip," she whispered to me.

After all these years, I still vividly recall sitting in her lap, warm and secure beneath a lap robe. Snow blanketed the countryside and the rhythmic trotting of the horse, the jingling of his harness and the steaming puffs of his breath floated on the crisp night air.

Christmas Day arrived and we went to my new grandmother's house where I met all the members of my new family. This Christmas ritual at grandmother's house was followed all through my younger years, a time of joy, love, and sharing.

May the grand lady who took me into her heart and home that long ago Christmas be forever blessed.

Preston Thompson
Tacoma, Washington

Country church

The Christmas I said my first Midnight Mass was in a small township in Wisconsin. The pastor of the main parish sent me to the mission parish with the instructions that "the people there will take care of things." When I arrived, the people assumed *I* would "take care of things." Ordained only six months and still finishing my studies, I had no ready ideas.

The singing was off-key, the "Silent Night" barely recognizable. A young teenager carried the statue of the Christ Child to the crib, stumbled, and fell, but held the statue aloft, shaking visibly. The other children in procession had no idea where to go or what to do. It was bitterly cold outside, the snow swirling, and the wind howling. The church was just adequately heated, but packed with heavily clothed, dairy-farm people. The smell of cattle hung heavy in the air. Responses to the Mass were definitely subdued.

My apprehension about my homily increased when the microphone ceased working. But eager faces strained to hear every word. At Communion time, the fervor of the people actually gave a glow to their weather-beaten faces.

After Mass, some parishioners stayed to drink coffee and hot cider. They talked about the beauty of the Mass and thanked me for driving sixty miles in the snow so they could have a Midnight Mass. Because one priest had to serve two parishes, it was the first time a Midnight Mass was celebrated in their church. Their love for the Mass, their gratitude and appreciation are still the best Christmas gift I ever received.

Thirty-eight years of Midnight Masses have not yet surpassed the joy of that first Midnight Mass.

Father Martin Stillmock, C.S.S.R.
Brooklyn Center, Minnesota

Something to do over again

I wish that I could go back to a childhood Christmas when I was about five years old and undo something I did.

I was the youngest of six children. I had decided that my life's ambition was to be a drummer like the man I used to watch in the band at the Slovak Hall. I loved music and wanted a drum set, so I asked for one for Christmas. Even though money was scarce in those Depression years, my parents didn't say no.

So that Christmas Eve, in our small four-room home, with our kitchen coal stove as our only available heat source, and our living room with its modest tree and trimmings, I was surprised with a drum set. But, to my great disappointment, it was a toy drum set, sold at the local five-&-ten-cent stores, not the real thing that my five-year-old imagination craved. Instead of shouting for joy and thanking my dear mother for her thoughtfulness and love in giving me this expensive gift, I cried and complained that it wasn't like the drums the drummer played at the dances. I don't remember even playing with it. I know my mother was hurt and let down by my reaction.

My mother is dead now. I don't remember ever discussing this with her. How I wish I could go back to that night and say "Thank you, Mom, you meant well, I love it and I love you for trying to make me happy." Perhaps sharing this story with others will make amends for my ungrateful behavior that holy Christmas Eve, many years ago.

Nicholas J. Novicky
Manville, New Jersey

Blind, but now I see

As Christmas approached that year, I wanted to find a hole and crawl into it. I had recently gone blind. It was the eighteenth of December. I hadn't decorated or done shopping. I saw no reds and greens, silver bells, or snow.

But then my husband, Paul, came home with four-year-old Michelle. She was from the orphanage, come to spend Christmas with us. We had had a child with us every year for the holidays. But not this year, I thought.

Yet, there she was, ours till January. I decided I'd go through the motions, for her. Michelle was a bright child, and she decided to help me. We decorated the tree with her advice as to where to hang the bulbs, as she described the colors to me. We laughed together!

We made cookies in shapes she constructed. She even helped me cook. Christmas morning, as she unwrapped her presents, she brought each for me to finger.

I saw Christmas through her eyes and as we went to church that day I really "saw" the holiday for the first time. It was glorious. Michelle became our adopted daughter six months later.

Ann Noha
Phoenix, Arizona

An adult's first Christmas

I have no happy Christmas memories from the first thirty years of my life. I came from a life of abuse and foster homes. I was passed around.

Then, when I was thirty, a lovely family brought me into their home as their daughter. It was an unbelievable Christmas to me, with a real live Christmas tree. I helped decorate the whole house and wrapped presents. My heart, which had been closed to the world outside, had opened to happiness and true love.

Just sitting, watching a "real" family together, was the way I dreamed it would be: each of us taking our turn in opening a present; the hugs and kisses at each gift. My heart felt full, with tree lights blinking, Christmas music playing, the train going around and around the tree — but most importantly the love that abounded from everyone, especially toward me. I felt wonderful and rich, something I had never experienced.

I think of that as my first Christmas. Each one since has been full of beautiful and wonderful memories, and a feeling of wholeness — something I had never had before.

Pauline A. Machan-Lewis
Mountain View, Missouri

All sixteen of us

It was Christmas season back in the '50s. Everyone was busy preparing with shopping, baking, and decorating our homes to celebrate the birth of our Savior.

Mom and Dad were looking forward to my husband and me and our five children spending Christmas day with them. My younger sister was home from college, so Mom and Dad would have two of their three children with them. Our kids consisted of teenagers on down to our three-year-old son. But there was always that sadness because our older sister and family from Pennsylvania lived so far away.

On Christmas Eve Mom and Dad had gone to bed. The snow was gently falling — perfect weather for this holy night.

A few hours later they were awakened by carolers singing right outside their bedroom window. Why would these singers come this late to a darkened house, where obviously its occupants were sleeping? Hurriedly, they made their way to the door to greet the carolers. When they opened the door, there stood my sister, her husband, and their four children.

Of all the Christmases I have spent with my parents, I have never seen them happier than when we gathered around the table for our dinner — all sixteen of us.

Kathryn Lozmack
Gallen, Michigan

Cruel trick

My parents were divorced, and for a while I lived in an orphanage. Christmas there was celebrated with a Santa (who I knew was not real) handing out bags of candy. When I was nine years old, my dad remarried. I was told we would spend Christmas with my stepmother's parents. They promised there would be snow, a Christmas tree, and real lights. Also, I could hang up my stocking on a real fireplace mantel.

My stepmother assured me Santa would fill my stocking with goodies. "Of course," she added, with a chuckle and glee in her eyes, "Santa leaves wooden sticks for bad boys and girls."

Sleep came slowly that night as I saw visions of a stocking full of candy, an orange or apple, and perhaps a doll or book. Finally, my stepmother was shaking me: "It's time to get up and see what Santa has brought." I quickly dressed and rushed to see the big surprise! My stocking was bulging — but not with goodies. Instead, it was wooden sticks. I was crushed, and tears began to well in my eyes. My stepmother laughed as I rushed from the room.

Years later I became a Catholic and learned how Jesus came into a cold, uncaring, unloving world. I could appreciate how Jesus became poor that I might become rich (see 2 Corinthians 8:9). Only God can turn our sorrows into joys and give us the perfect gift of His Son.

Now Christmas is a thrill because I have the privilege of attending Christmas Midnight Mass, where the real heavenly Father gives us the most perfect Christmas gift of His Son, Jesus.

Theresa Black
Necedah, Wisconsin

Bright star shining

The years were 1928 through 1930. We lived in Bartlesville, Oklahoma, and my father and older brother worked for the Santa Fe Railroad as laborers. Fortunately they didn't get laid off, although they were reduced to half-days in the worst times.

Their combined wages furnished us with beans, tortillas, and the bare necessities of life. We lived in a rent-free railroad house made out of railroad ties and assorted lumber and cardboard, with numerous cracks and leaks that let the winter winds blow in. An older brother, Paul, and I attended St. John's Catholic school taught by the Ursuline Sisters of Paoli, Kansas. Tuition was one dollar per month per child.

Our Christmas schedule was for Paul and me to serve midnight Mass for Father Hubert Van Recium (from Belgium) along with eight other boys, and then to be fortunate enough to be picked to serve the two low Masses that immediately followed.

These Masses were very short; Father could breeze through the Latin in about twenty minutes each. Then we would hurry home where our mother, Soledad, would give us hot chocolate and cookies. Paul would then sleep about three hours and get up at five-thirty to help the local Lions Club deliver reconditioned Christmas toys to what we considered were really poor families.

As we walked and ran home after the three Masses in the bitter cold, the stars seemed so close and unusually bright! We kept looking for the Christmas Star of Bethlehem. We knew that even though we were materially poor, our inside feelings told us that we had everything! After all,

having just received the Christ Child in Holy Communion and attended three Masses, what else was there?
We had it all!

Joseph G. Gamino
Oklahoma City, Oklahoma

Confirmed

When I was ten years old, I spent Halloween night with my friend, Herbie Allen. Very early the next morning, his mother awakened us to announce we had to hurry or we would be late for seven a.m. Mass. I said, "But it's not Sunday." Sleepily, Herbie said he knew that, but it was All Saints' Day and a holy day of obligation. None of this made sense to a little Baptist boy, but I hurried and went with them as if I knew why.

On the way, Herbie and Mrs. Allen explained, or tried to, what the significance of the day was. It was the first time I had ever been inside a Catholic church. Naturally, I was impressed with the church's interior — the statues, candles, and stained-glass windows. But I think the sincere devotion of the communicants impressed me most.

When I was fifteen, I joined the Episcopal Church. I was a "good Episcopalian," working in and for my parish for many years. Yet all the while, I could only find complete solace and devotion attending a Catholic church.

Finally, at age thirty-nine, I took instructions to join the Catholic Church with a wonderful Jesuit pastor of Sacred Heart Church in Hollywood, California. One day I asked when I could be confirmed. Father said not until the bishop visited during Easter. I said that I really didn't want to wait, that I wanted to receive Communion at the Christmas Midnight Mass. Father did not say anything.

Several days later, on December 23, Father called to ask me to some to the rectory at three p.m. There in the rectory's private chapel, on December 23, 1975, I was confirmed and at long last felt that I had achieved spiritual completeness.

Never had Christmas meant so much to me as when I went up to the altar and received Our Lord, two days after my confirmation. I am reminded of that blessed Christmas almost every time I approach the altar for Communion.

C. J. Thomason
Fort Worth, Texas

A Canadian letter

A week before Christmas 1962 we piled our children, ranging in age from two to eight, into an aging station wagon, and headed for the store parking lot to shop for just-the-right tree at just-the-right price.

Of course, the most perfect trees were too high, not just height-wise, but also budget-wise, and Mom and Dad contrived one excuse or another to discourage the kiddies' first selections. Eventually, a compromise was made, and Dad knew that with a branch sawed off here and wired in there, this tree would please even Mom's sense of artistic balance.

During this cosmetic tree surgery we discovered a little plastic bag tied to the trunk. Inside was a folded piece of paper. It was a note in a child's handwriting:

"To whoever finds this. My father and mother and my sister and me live in the country, and my father cuts trees. My mother and my baby sister stay home, and I help him. We are poor, so we won't have much for Christmas, so if you find this, could you send a toy for my sister? My father gets food for the family, but not any toys. Thank you."

After much discussion, we decided that the children would reduce their wish lists for Santa so that we could go shopping for our adopted family. In just two days we piled into the station wagon once again, this time to the post office to mail Santa's gifts to our unknown Canadians friends.

We received a very heartfelt "thank you" note shortly after the New Year. The memory has lasted, and now our grandchildren hear this story and look for a little plastic bag tied to the trunk whenever they shop for their Christmas tree.

Mrs. G. R. Boudreaux
Metairie, Louisiana

The reunion

I remember my first Christmas in Catholic school and being taught by the Sisters of St. Joseph. The sisters wanted to put on a Christmas pageant, and I and my childhood sweetheart were to play the parts of Mary and Joseph.

The sisters encouraged us, and we were fairly obedient children, but our exuberance often caused us to talk during the school sessions and pay less attention to our classwork.

It was during one of these times that I was reprimanded for talking in class and was demoted from playing the part of the Blessed Mother to an angel who appeared to the shepherds while watching their flocks. I learned my lines faithfully, although I was heartbroken over not being able to play the part of Mary. In my heart I felt I would never forgive the sister who robbed me of my childhood dream.

Many years went by and I drifted away from the Church and my religion, but always at Christmas I would be able to repeat those lines spoken by the angel to the shepherds. After nearly twenty years of tepid faith and religion, I experienced a wonderful conversion, which brought me back into the Church community as an active participant in parish work.

I wondered where that sister was, and if she were still alive today. God in His great love would not let me forget her. I made several inquiries, and surprisingly enough she was still living in a city not far from my hometown. I went to see her. She had not forgotten me, and had always regretted having to punish me for talking in class when I was just a precocious child. We hugged each other and since that day have become the best of friends, spending much time together.

Julianna M. Connolly
West Lynn, Massachusetts

A prayer for Dad

As Christmas drew closer, my three sisters and I searched earnestly for gifts for the dearest and most important man in our lives, our dad. Mom and I helped the young ones wrap the packages, and guided little fingers to print "with love" on the pretty tags.

My dad celebrated in his own way; his holiday spirit came in a bottle. By Christmas morning, he'd have a terrible headache and be mean and sarcastic with all of us. But what he did with his gifts was the worst. He refused to open them. In an ugly, black mood, he ignored the pretty packages with the lovely notes and just left them under the tree.

After several days, mom unwrapped the gifts and put them away. Eventually, Dad wore the new shirt, read the new book, and smelled like the new after-shave lotion. He never said "Thank you."

Years went by before I was able to forgive my father for the many hurts he caused his young daughters. The pain left when I gratefully accepted God's wonderful Christmas present, the One who removed the shameful, harmful sin of hate from my life. Christmas now means hope, not heartache.

My continuous prayer is that my stubborn old dad will not continue to turn his back on the most important gift ever.

Name Withheld
Kenner, Louisiana

An alcoholic's Christmas

As a child my father was an active alcoholic and the only day he never drank (shook yes, but drank no) was Christmas Day. I always waited each year with great anticipation for Christmas Day, for it was the only day I didn't have a knot in my gut. I always felt safe on this day. With God's grace and love and many years of prayer, my father stopped drinking and obtained a great amount of peace, love, and sobriety.

I was to start my drinking at seventeen years old and continue for twenty-five years. It ruined my life and I reached great depths of personal hell. I could not stop no matter how hard I tried. Again God reached out and touched my life. For on the Christmas before I stopped drinking, I thought I would die and asked Him for help. It came two months later through His grace and love, and I too found sobriety.

The Christmases that have followed have been absolutely beautiful, for I feel like I did as a child. Only now each and every day is like Christmas. I feel safe, I feel totally spiritual, I feel wanted, I feel needed, and above all, I feel loved.

William McCoy
Pine Plaines, New York

Homeless at the holidays

At Christmas 1990, my husband and I were separated because of alcohol abuse and financial difficulties. My son Joey and I were staying in Safehome, a shelter for homeless women and children. I entered Safehome confused, depressed, worried, and frightened. Immediately, I was greeted by warm voices and friendly hearts. Joey and I were given all the clothes, food, medicine, and shelter we needed. Everyone listened to my problems and then helped me to work out the solutions. I was given all the legal and financial aid and advice needed at that moment.

Safehome gave Joey and me a beautiful Christmas. He received all the books, toys, and stuffed animals that any nineteen-month-old boy could desire. I received clothes, perfume, and all sorts of beautiful feminine items.

My husband and I have both since kicked the alcohol, and our family is back together. We have learned to live one day at a time and to listen to God. I learned that God really does answer prayers if we only open our eyes, ears, and hearts to Him.

Now I drop those extra dollars — when possible — in the church basket or charity basket. I know now from experience, and am very grateful for, the help these organization offer the homeless during Christmas.

Robin M. Riddle
Kansas City, Missouri

Our Sunday Visitor...
Your Source for Discovering the Riches of the Catholic Faith

Our Sunday Visitor has an extensive line of materials for young children, teens, and adults. Our books, Bibles, booklets, CD-ROMs, audios, and videos are available in bookstores worldwide.

To receive a FREE full-line catalog or for more information, call **Our Sunday Visitor** at **1-800-348-2440**. Or write, **Our Sunday Visitor** / 200 Noll Plaza / Huntington, IN 46750.

Please send me: __ A catalog
Please send me materials on:
    __ Apologetics and catechetics   __ Reference works
    __ Prayer books   __ Heritage and the saints
    __ The family   __ The parish

Name_____
Address_____Apt._____
City_____State___Zip_____
Telephone (   )_____

A73BBABP

Please send a friend: __ A catalog
Please send a friend materials on:
    __ Apologetics and catechetics   __ Reference works
    __ Prayer books   __ Heritage and the saints
    __ The family   __ The parish

Name_____
Address_____Apt._____
City_____State___Zip_____
Telephone (   )_____

A73BBABP

Our Sunday Visitor
200 Noll Plaza
Huntington, IN 46750
1-800-348-2440
OSVSALES@AOL.COM

Your Source for Discovering the Riches of the Catholic Faith